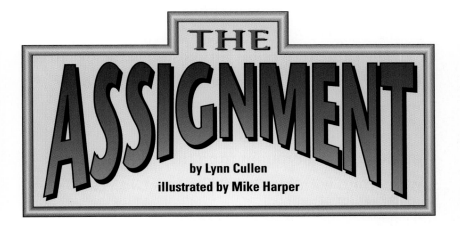

THE ASSIGNMENT

by Lynn Cullen

illustrated by Mike Harper

MODERN CURRICULUM PRESS
Pearson Learning Group

Tyler pushed his bedroom door closed and shouted, "Go away!"

The thin voice of his little sister, Nancy, pierced through the door. "I just want to come in for a minute. I won't touch anything, I promise!"

"Go away. I'm busy," said Tyler. He bit into the apple he'd just brought from the kitchen. What was wrong with his sister? She was two years younger than he and always sneaking into his room.Tyler dropped onto his bed. He stared at the assignment sheet next to him on the bed. Unfortunately, a miracle had not happened. A bolt of lightning had not come down out of the sky and struck Ms. Gump's words from the sheet. Fire had not flared up and destroyed the paper. A flood had not washed in through his window. His assignment was still there, and it was due on Monday.

3

Glumly, Tyler read it again.

For our Oregon Trail Unit, please choose from the following three exercises:

1) *Write an essay about life as a pioneer on the Oregon Trail. Explain why you would or would not have liked to have been a pioneer.*

Tyler groaned through clenched teeth. More writing! Ms. Gump was crazy about writing, making her students write essays on everything from presidents to pelicans. He'd written enough words to fill a large book. He took another bite of his apple. If only he could write as well as he ate. He had an excellent appetite.

He looked at the next choice on the assignment sheet.

2) *Make an advertising flyer for a good wagon and its contents. Be sure to show all of the items settlers would have taken with them on the trail.*

Tyler crunched into his apple, thinking. He liked drawing, but it didn't like him. His stick figures looked just like that—sticks—not people.

Only last week he'd decorated his report on the Plains Indians with hand-drawn pictures of Native Americans riding their horses.

Ms. Gump had looked at his illustration and frowned. "What do dogs chasing sticks have to do with the Plains Indians?" she had asked.

Tyler went on to exercise number three.

3) *Make a food the pioneers would have eaten while on the trail, and be prepared to tell about it. Bring enough to share with the class.*

Tyler chewed his apple more slowly. Maybe this one wasn't so bad. If he cooked something, at least he would have the pleasure of eating it.

His door opened. A curly head eased into sight. "Tyler?" said Nancy.

Tyler dropped his assignment sheet onto the bed. "What do you want?"

"Will you play a game with me?"

"A game!" Tyler exclaimed. "That will take too long. I've got important stuff to do. Out."

With a sigh, Nancy closed the door.

Tyler shook his head. Did he ever nag Nancy? Never. In fact, since he had started fifth grade, he had pretty much ignored her. Why was she always pestering him?

He snatched up the assignment sheet. What could he make for his pioneer food? He couldn't cook just anything. It had to be authentic. If it wasn't a real pioneer food, Ms. Gump would know it. And Tyler couldn't afford a bad grade.

His report with the drawing that looked like Native American dogs and their sticks had earned him a D. Several of his other essays had not done much better. If he got any more grades like that on his next report card, his mother would make him drop soccer. That would be a tragedy. Tyler liked soccer almost as much as he liked eating.

Tyler finished his apple and dropped the core into his sweatshirt pocket. First he had to figure out what foods the pioneers ate. He bent over the side of his bed and rummaged through his backpack until he found his social studies book. He hauled it into his lap and looked up the chapter on the Oregon Trail. Running his finger over the pages, he skimmed the paragraphs. At last he found a mention of meat. He backtracked and read slowly.

The pioneers had a limited diet. Besides coffee and bread, they consumed what they could scavenge on the trail. Buffalo meat was most commonly eaten, usually dried as a jerky.

Tyler frowned. Why couldn't the pioneers eat yummy pastries or something? Where was he going to get his hands on buffalo meat? And he sure didn't want to eat it—dried or not. There had to be something else he could cook.

A knock sounded on the door.

"Who is it?" he called.

"Me." It was Nancy.

"I told you to go away," said Tyler.

"Want to come outside and kick around the soccer ball with me?" she asked through the door.

Tyler sighed. Kicking the soccer ball—even with his little sister—sounded better than working on this assignment. Still, it was Thursday afternoon and the project was due Monday. He didn't want to spend his whole weekend slaving away. If he was lucky, he and the guys would go to a movie tomorrow night. And Saturday he had a soccer game.

"I can't play now, Nancy," he said, making his voice sound as pitiful as he felt. "I've got to go to the library."

The door swung open. "You do?" Nancy asked Tyler. "Good. I'll go too."

Before Tyler could answer, Nancy was skipping to the kitchen. "Mom," she called, "Tyler has to go to the library. Can you drive us there now?"

Tyler could hear his mother's voice in the kitchen. "I've got to start dinner, Nancy, and I've worked all day. I'm exhausted."

Even from his room, Tyler heard the weariness in his mother's tone. He lay back on his bed. They weren't going anywhere soon. When Mom was tired, the world came to a stop. He'd probably be stuck going to the library tomorrow. Maybe he'd even miss the movie.

"But Mom, Tyler has to go," came Nancy's voice from the kitchen now. "It's important. Don't worry. I'll help you make dinner when we get back. What are we having?"

To Tyler's surprise, Mom said, "Lasagna. I guess I can put it off for a half hour, as long as you'll help me."

Soon Tyler was sitting in the back seat of the family station wagon, still wondering how Nancy had talked Mom into going to the library.

Inside the library, Tyler went straight to the front desk. He tried to ignore Nancy. "I need some books about the Oregon Trail, please," he told the librarian.

The librarian, a young woman with black hair down to her waist, smiled. "No problem. See those computer terminals over there?" She pointed to a row of booths. "Every book we own is listed on computer. All you have to do is type in *Oregon Trail* next to the place on the screen marked 'Subject.' It will tell you the book and the Dewey decimal number under which you can find it."

Tyler tried not to let the librarian see him scowling. He'd hoped she would find the book for him. The librarians usually did. He walked over to the nearest terminal.

"I'll show you," piped up Nancy, hanging over his shoulder.

"I know what I'm doing," Tyler said, though he had never used any of the terminals.

"Use the mouse to point to the picture marked 'catalog,' " said Nancy.

Tyler clicked onto "catalog." A new screen appeared, offering the choices of "Titles," "Subject/Title Words," and "Author/Performer." Tyler pointed the cursor to "Subject/Title Words," and typed in *Oregon Trail*. A list of books filled the screen.

"Click on one of the titles," said Nancy. "It'll tell you more about it."

"I know, I know," said Tyler.

He clicked on a book listing. He read the short description of the book that flashed on the screen. "That sounds good."

Nancy shook her head, making her curls bounce. "If you want the book tonight, that one won't work. That book's at another library." She pointed to a line marked "Holdings." "See? This one's at the North Lake Branch."

"Oh," said Tyler.

Tyler returned to the list of books on the Oregon Trail. He chose the next book.

"Great," said Nancy, before Tyler had started reading the entry. "It's here. It's Dewey decimal number is J979.503 Bro. The 'Bro' stands for the author, Julius Brown. The 979.503 is where all the stuff on the Oregon Trail is put. The 'J' means it's a kid's book." She took off for the kids' section.

Tyler followed Nancy, looking around to make sure no one saw him trailing after his little sister. In the children's section, Nancy marched past two rows of shelves. She pointed to the sign at the end of the row printed with the words "Juvenile Nonfiction." Below the sign were numbers and arrows. "See?" she said. "J940 to J999. This way."

She scuttled along the row of books, pointing at the numbers on the bottom of the books' spines. She came to a halt and pulled out a thin volume with a picture of a covered wagon on front. "Here it is."

Tyler frowned. "How did you learn to do all this?"

Nancy shrugged. "I listen to the librarian when my class goes to the media center."

"Oh," said Tyler.

Whenever Tyler's class had lessons in the media center, he used the time to catch up on homework. It made the librarian mad, but he figured that if he did his homework in school, he would have more time to play soccer after school. Now he wished he'd listened more closely. He didn't enjoy being shown up by a third grader.

He took the book from Nancy. She peered over his shoulder as he flipped through it.

"Why don't you look in the index?" she asked.

Tyler glared as he turned to the back of the book. "Are you happy now?"

"What's your subject?" asked Nancy.

"Food."

Nancy looked at her brother. Then she laughed. "Big surprise!"

Tyler clenched his jaw. "I'm supposed to find out what the pioneers ate on the Oregon Trail, okay? Then I've got to cook it for my class."

Nancy struggled to press the smile from her lips. She nodded.

Tyler followed the index entries until he found "food." "All right! It's here."

"What page number?" asked Nancy.

"Nineteen to twenty," said Tyler, not waiting for her to tell him to look it up. He found page twenty first and immediately began to read.

The next stop for the wagon train was at noon, for a quick meal of dried meat. Most families ate this meal standing up. Business that needed to be done with other members of the party was often done at this time.

The wagon train hit the trail by two, not stopping until almost dark. Then the wagons drew around in a tight circle and fires were started. Now came the largest meal of the day. A typical dinner might consist of beans and dried meat, or if wild game was available, buffalo or antelope steaks, or perhaps stewed prairie chicken.

Tyler sagged. "More buffalo meat. I can't cook any of this."

"Let me see," said Nancy.

Tyler listlessly handed her the book. Now he would have to spend his entire weekend trying to come up with a stew that tasted like prairie chicken. He would never get to go to the movie tomorrow night. He'd have to spend the time at the grocery, shopping for little chickens. Saturday, he'd have to leave his soccer game the second it ended to come home to stew the tiny creatures. And what was stewing, anyway?

Nancy flipped back a page from where Tyler had stopped and read silently to herself. She read the passage slowly, stopping on a word here and there. At last she said, "Tyler, did you read this?"

The book clenched in his hand, Tyler read the last paragraph of page nineteen to himself.

The pioneers started their day at six o'clock in the morning. Breakfast consisted of coffee, sowbelly (bacon), and flapjacks or cornbread, which they cooked in a pan over an open fire. By seven, all wagons were packed and ready to roll.

Tyler looked up. "We're way too young for coffee, and I'm not making bacon and calling it sowbelly. Everyone will laugh."

"No, silly," said Nancy. "What about cornbread?"

Tyler stared at his sister. His mother made cornbread. It tasted pretty good, especially with honey. He'd seen his mother make it lots of times. She used cornmeal, milk, eggs, and some grease for the pan. In fact, there was a bag of cornmeal in the cupboard right now.

Tyler knew this because he had knocked the bag over this morning, when he had gotten out some brown sugar for his cereal.

"I wouldn't even have to go to the store," said Tyler. "We already have everything to make it at home. Even the cornmeal." He pumped his fist. "Yes!"

Later, on the way home, after Tyler had checked out the book, he sat in the front seat of the car, planning his weekend. He'd call his friends when he got home and start lining up rides to the movie theater tomorrow. Thank goodness Nancy had helped him find a food for his project. She'd gotten him out of a bind.

He turned toward the back seat. "Hey, Nancy. Do you want to help me make the cornbread?"

Nancy shook her head. "I won't have time. Your book gave me an idea. I want to start an Oregon Trail Club. I'm going to call Carol and Milly when we get home. We can make pioneer things and pretend we're on the Oregon Trail."

"That sounds nice, Nancy," said Mom.

"Come on, Nancy" said Tyler. "You like cornbread and honey. I'll let you have a little bit."

"Thanks," said Nancy, "but I won't need any. I can make all the cornbread we want—flapjacks and sowbelly too. I'm going to have all my friends over tomorrow. Is that okay, Mom?"

Tyler's mother nodded. "Sounds lovely."

Tyler groaned. What had he done? Now instead of having one little pest around, he'd have bunches.

Nancy leaned forward and kissed him on the arm. "I love you, Tyler."

Tyler sighed. He had to admit that for a pesky third-grade sister, the kid was pretty smart.